CONTINUING
THE CONVERSATION

—— *Selected Writings* ——

ARCHBISHOP PHILIP FREIER

COVENTRY
PRESS

Published in Australia by
Coventry Press
33 Scoresby Road
Bayswater VIC 3153

ISBN 9781922589620

Copyright © Philip Freier 2025

All rights reserved. Other than for the purposes and subject to the conditions prescribed under the Copyright Act, no part of this publication may be reproduced, stored in a retrieval system, or transmitted in any form or by any means, electronic, mechanical, photocopying, recording or otherwise, without the prior permission of the publisher.

Catalogue-in-Publication entry is available from the National Library of Australia
http://catalogue.nla.gov.au

Cover design by Ian James – www.jgd.com.au
Cover image by Eugene Hyland (2015)
Used by permission of Newspix
Text design by Coventry Press
Set in EB Garamond

Printed in Australia 2025

Contents

A Prayer for Melbourne
  Archbishop Freier xi

Foreword
  Mark Brolly xiii

Preface
  Archbishop Freier xvii

Community encounters challenge us all to listen
  March 2007 1

The ethics of stem cell research
  April 2007 4

Let's cherish the rights we take for granted
  May 2008 7

Walking for Millennium Development Goals
  September 2008 10

True faith requires us to trust that all will be well
  June 2009 13

Welcome must be more than 'hello' at the door
  August 2009 15

Deeper wisdom of faith could challenge knife violence
  March 2010 18

Perfect love casts out fear
  June 2010 20

'Comfort them, Lord, in this disaster'
March 2011 22

Valuing Indigenous knowledge in contemporary society
August 2011 26

The power of a constitutional framework for the national church
May 2012 28

Lessons learned in a life of radical commitment to holiness
November 2012 30

God's abiding love remains a haven against violence
December 2013 32

Australia's Indigenous and non-Indigenous – equal in God's eyes
June 2014 34

The new Primate calls for fervent prayer
September 2014 36

An ordered society, evidence of God's hand
September 2015 38

The gift of seeing criticism as divine blessing
November 2015 40

Bombs can never destroy Christ's love for us
April 2016 42

'Such love, filling my emptiness... O Jesus, such love'
June 2016 44

We must own our past – both good and bad
August 2016 46

The need for constitutional recognition
November 2017 48

Wailing, grief and hope as a life is remembered
March 2018 50

Walking together, despite our divisions
May 2018 52

Honouring George Freier and all the fallen of WWI
June 2018 53

From times of crisis, deeper faith can emerge
July 2019 55

Seek light, give thanks, don't dwell in shadows
September 2019 57

Cosmic calling with Christ a way ahead on climate
February 2020 59

'Forgotten blessings' rediscovered in lockdown
July 2020 61

Time for a relevant national anthem
November 2020 63

Thinking about the soul
August 2021 65

No room for complacency
November 2021 67

Prayers for first steps towards reimagining future
August 2022 69

On our doors, at our tables, we can share God's gift to us
December 2022 72

Contemplating the divine vision of Jubilee
June 2023 74

Abide in Jesus, not outrage culture
August 2023 76

The Yoorook Justice Commission and our Diocese's painful history
June 2024 78

Love of neighbour
July 2024 80

A Prayer for Melbourne

God of community,
    We give you thanks for this beautiful and vibrant city:
    for its diversity of people and cultural life,
    for its industry and commerce,
    for its hospitals and agencies of care,
    and its places of learning, recreation and worship.

God of compassion,
    We pray for all who live and work in this city and for those who visit her:
    open our hearts to welcome the stranger,
    shelter the homeless, befriend the lonely, care for the needy and offer hope to those in despair,
    for these are your people.

This prayer was written in November 2007, at the end of Rev. Dr Philip Freier's first year in office as Archbishop. It resulted from his Prayer4Melbourne quest... a year long journey of visiting parts of Melbourne and Geelong, getting to know this city that he was to then serve for 18 years. The prayer was launched at a special event at Federation Square.

Foreword

An enduring legacy in difficult times

It is an honour, though a daunting one, to be invited to reflect on Archbishop Philip Freier's retirement after leading the Melbourne diocese for 18 years. Not as daunting, surely, as it must have been for Philip and Joy Freier when he was enthroned in December 2006. They had spent their lives in Australia's north, much of it in Far North Queensland and then for seven years in Darwin where he was Bishop of the Northern Territory until his election as Melbourne's 13th Anglican leader since 1847.

One measure of Philip Freier's legacy is to recall the state of church and nation in late 2006. He was the fifth Anglican Archbishop of Melbourne in the less than 30 years since Sir Frank Woods had retired after his 20-year episcopate here.

As the Freiers take their leave, only Charles Perry and Frank Woods have led the diocese for longer. Lambeth Palace as well as Bishopscourt are awaiting new residents after Rowan Williams' successor, Justin Welby, resigned as Archbishop of Canterbury amid controversy. And there have been seven changes of Prime Minister and five of Premier since that day at St Paul's Cathedral when Philip Freier took office.

Archbishop Freier advanced the cause of women's ordination when, in 2008, he consecrated Barbara Darling as Melbourne's first female bishop, shortly after Victorian Kay Goldsworthy had become Australia's first in Perth.

Two of the greatest challenges in his time have been the child sexual abuse crisis, with successive inquiries by a Victorian parliamentary committee and by the 2013-17 Royal Commission into Institutional Responses to Child Sexual Abuse; and the global coronavirus pandemic from 2020, which closed down so much of life, including public worship and much ministry. Their impact is far from over or even fully understood.

Archbishop Freier hit the ground running in Melbourne through programs such as Prayer4Melbourne, visiting workplaces and shopping centres to find out what mattered to people and what concerns they thought the Church should be praying about.

In 2010, he launched a plan to make the Word of God fully known across the entire diocese, leading to efforts to renew parishes and the establishment of the Bishop Perry Institute to coordinate training and resourcing efforts.

His longest-running and perhaps most memorable public engagement was through his Breakfast Conversations with guests involved in issues of public importance such as toxic childhoods, climate change, asylum seekers, the changing nature of family relationships, mental health and politics. Guests included former Prime Minister Malcolm Fraser, social researcher Hugh Mackay, historian Janet McCalman, First Nations leader Marcia Langton and Anglicare Victoria CEO Paul McDonald. Poignantly, Archbishop Freier's final guest in October had been one of his first, Michael Leunig, the cartoonist, artist and public prophet who died just before Christmas.

From 2014-20, Dr Freier served as Primate, only the third Melbourne Anglican leader to do so after Archbishops Woods and Keith Rayner. He has had other international roles, such as co-Chair of the Anglican-Roman Catholic International Commission.

But it was the concerns of the original inhabitants of Australia, whom Philip Freier has sought to serve as a layman, priest and bishop for more than 40 years, to which he often turned. In 2023, the referendum to enshrine a Voice for First Nations people to Parliament in the Constitution was soundly defeated. In his final Presidential Address to Synod last October, Dr Freier reiterated the words of his first Synod Charge in 2007 that national concern for Aboriginal people should be lasting, 'authentic, generous, and sympathetic; that it will genuinely seek the very best outcomes for Aboriginal people – the outcomes they themselves want'. May Archbishop and Mrs Freier and their family enjoy good health and happiness in retirement.

Mark Brolly
Formerly, journalist, *The Melbourne Anglican*

Preface

A month can seem a long time, or, if you have a publishing deadline to meet, a short time! It is interesting for me to look back over the almost 200 short pieces of writing that constitute my efforts of communication each month to the readers of *The Melbourne Anglican*, the TMA. A multi award-winning church publication, the TMA takes a broad view of what is important in the Church and in the world. It has a committed readership base that is wider than just the members of the Diocese of Melbourne. I have valued the discipline of this monthly writing task and have enjoyed reflecting on what I would write in the weeks preceding the monthly deadline.

Over the same period, I had about 60 'Conversations with the Archbishop' at the Edge, a theatre space in Federation Square, just opposite St Paul's Cathedral. These were broadly on the theme, 'What kind of society do we want?' My TMA words were necessarily different from these discussions as they were responding to the questions, 'What kind of Church does God want in our time?' and 'What kind of Christian discipleship is needed for our age?'

For those who have been kind enough to tell me that my words were the first thing they turned to each month, I hope this publication will carry a sense of the world and the Church over these past eighteen years. Who knows? Perhaps a second reading will give some fresh insight to the questions I have posed that remain vital for God's mission in the world. For those who encounter these words for the first time, I pray that they will be an encouragement to more deeply consider the claims of God upon each of us.

Archbishop Philip Freier

Community encounters challenge us all to listen

This month I embarked on my Prayer4Melbourne quest, a time of engaging with the people of Melbourne where they are, visiting public spaces to hear about their concerns and prayers for this expansive and multicultural city. The quest is an extraordinary privilege for me. To ask people to share their heart's longings is a big request.

While it is certainly important that as a Christian leader I am informed about the place that I'm in so that I can pray for the people and the community, I have also felt constantly humbled by Melburnians' willingness to share their lives, their hopes, and their worries with me.

Perhaps it's because I'm not selling something, or perhaps it's because I look distinctive in my purple bishop's shirt and cross, but I continue to be amazed by how warmly people receive me.

In trips to various shopping centres, including Fountain Gate in the South East, Airport West in what one person described as 'the forgotten West' and Glenferrie Road in the more prosperous inner suburb of Hawthorn, I have encountered people who have come from many different backgrounds. Two students who came to Melbourne from North India alerted me to what an important education centre Melbourne is, and how safe they felt here. I met three older Italians who are appalled by the soccer violence in their home country. I have met people from Sri Lanka, Samoa, Ethiopia, Scotland, Romania, Slovenia, Greece, Cyprus, Italy and Malta. I have met Catholics, Anglicans, Hindus and Pentecostalists. We are a multicultural city and it is a privilege to be serving in its midst.

I have also heard deep concerns about the challenges facing all of us in the community. Parents have expressed to me their concern to spend quality time with their children, and their fears of the influence of drugs. Felice and Tracy from Craigieburn explained how Felice, concerned about the demands of his job stopping him from actively fathering his four young children, has elected to start his own business. What amazing courage.

Barb is troubled by her inability to find a day placement program for her daughter Tara, a mentally disabled woman in need of age-appropriate companionship and activity. A widower told me how in his loneliness he goes to Fountain Gate shopping centre regularly just for the human contact. The lack of such community resources is placing a burden not just on Barb and Tara but many families in our state. Families have written to me to express concern about the lack of facilities for their disabled adult children and their increasing inability to care for them as they age. If this is an issue for you, I would ask you to also write to me, as I am keen to understand this issue better.

The conversations I have had have been very helpful in encouraging me to be thankful to God for the blessings of life and the community I share. As I have walked and drank coffee, talked and listened, the recurring theme for me was that Jesus, God who became human, came to earth for all of us – for those who are grieving and in pain, the refugees, the disabled and the able bodies, and just ordinary people who wake up each day feeling lonely and sad.

This is a challenge for all of us. If we reached out to our neighbour or if we allowed our neighbour to reach out to us, we would indeed become a community and not isolated individuals visiting shopping centres.

When my Prayer4Melbourne quest has concluded, I intend to write a prayer for Melbourne, which will be publicly released, encompassing the stories I have been told and the hopes that have been expressed to me. In the meantime, I would encourage each of us not just to acknowledge our own stories, but to listen intently to the stories of those around us. Be prepared to be humbled and in awe of your neighbours and friends as they share their past and their hopes and concerns for the future.

March 2007

The ethics of stem cell research

I have been concerned with the vexed ethical questions surrounding the legislation to allow therapeutic cloning which was passed in the Federal Parliament late last year, and the similar legislation which was presented to the Victorian Parliament in early March of this year.

The ethics of embryonic stem cell research are challenging and complex. I have respect for the position of the Roman Catholic Church – and of many in the Anglican Church – that all human life from the moment of conception is sacred and has an inviolable right to life. From this basis a range of other moral questions are more readily answered than if that foundational matter is left unresolved.

However, it is not my intention here in this short article to try to establish whether the Roman Catholic ethical system is right or wrong in its entirety, but rather to pose some of the questions which need to be asked and to seek a broad perspective on the ethical debate which surrounds stem cell research.

While the stem cells issue is important, we also need to remember that at the current time there are disturbing threats to the sacredness of human life which cry out for urgent attention and justice – in many countries violence, war, poverty, and oppression are blighting the lives of millions. One billion people live on under $2 a day. 100 people are dying each day in Iraq as a result of war. Global warming and climate change threaten the livelihoods of many, particularly in poor countries, as well as the very future of the planet itself.

Perhaps the most critical and contentious question the stem cells debate raises is, at what point does human life begin? Is being able to think and feel like a human being the test or is it just having the potential to develop these abilities? But if we decide a cluster of cells just days old – the early pre-implantation embryo does not satisfy this criterion, then what do we say about an old person with severe dementia – and is this person any less human than a fit and healthy young person?

Is it possible to say we are more or less human at different points on the continuum of life? Or do we have an essential and indivisible humanness which remains the same at every point?

Is it reasonable for the opponents of the legislation to argue emotively on the grounds that it allows human life to be created and then to be 'killed off'?

A vital question for Christians is, What does it mean to be made in the image of God? Are we made in this image simply through our DNA and biological distinctiveness, or does it depend on our becoming human persons in relationship with God?

The legislation allows for experimentation on the embryo up to 14 days. However, what are the guarantees and safeguards that this time will not be extended in the future? After all, abortions may be performed beyond this time.

Some have argued that therapeutic cloning is in reality no different from reproductive cloning. They assert that the only difference is that under the proposed legislation the renucleated egg will be destroyed. It is not implausible to imagine that in the future pressure may be brought from scientists or society to amend the legislation so it may be possible to implant such an embryo, for example, in a woman whose spouse may be dying, and who would see this as an opportunity to produce a child who was genetically the same as the spouse.

Also, how long would it be before scientists would be able to produce the 'perfect' embryo, with the prospect of good looks and a high IQ?

There is no doubt that the legislation has been proposed from the noblest humanitarian and compassionate motives, both among politicians and scientists, and that there is potential for great good in the legislation, with the possibility of finding cures – even if these may be decades off – for some terrible diseases.

At the same time it would be naïve to pretend that for some the commercial benefits which may flow from the research have not been a motivating factor in supporting the legislation.

While the desire to reduce human suffering is no doubt the chief motivation for many, and this is only to be commended, serious questions remain about this issue, and we cannot ignore the possibility that in the future it may develop in ways which may be even more ethically problematical. I think that we are facing the situation where the issue is one of acquiring this knowledge with all of the ethical uncertainties it presents or agreeing to limit such research in the interests of greater ethical integrity.

April 2007

Let's cherish the rights we take for granted

When did you last have a sense of appreciation as you headed off to church on Sunday, appreciation, that is, of your freedom to do so? Recently at the Parish of St Aidan's, Noble Park, I observed a congregation of worshippers, some of whom were Sudanese and whose life stories include religious persecution amongst other traumatic experiences. Scarcely imaginable to us from more peaceful countries, the lack of freedom for Christians to worship openly is common in many parts of our 21st century world. The almost tangible joyful spirit of the Sudanese worship must surely be enhanced by the knowledge that here in Australia we have the right publicly to come together as Christians and to proclaim the name of Jesus Christ as Saviour and Lord.

In Australia, we are fortunate that belief in God is permitted to be a matter of conscience and freewill. This is not universally the case, even though the sway of the compulsory atheism of various totalitarian regimes appears to be waning throughout the world. In our Anzac services we saluted those who at their own cost defended our freedoms, ensuring what we take for granted today.

My March Breakfast Conversation with Human Rights lawyer and advocate Julian Burnside raised the issue of a Bill of Rights for Australia. Perhaps this idea emerged at the Canberra 2020 Summit; whatever, the rights we already enjoy as part of a democratic society are to be cherished. There is talk again of the monarchy vs republic debate and a possible referendum. If so, we may or may not each be satisfied with the outcome but our right to go to the ballot boxes without fear of reprisal or intimidation cannot be overstated.

With the impending consecrations of women bishops comes a different matter of rights or, rather, expectations. While I with the majority of the Diocese am personally delighted that we will have women in the Episcopate, I feel the pain of those who do not believe in the ordination of women. Our right to worship according to our conscience and the formularies of the Church is critical. Together with the Council of the Diocese I will endeavour to ensure that there is proper provision for those who cannot in conscience receive the ministry of women. To that end, I will be initiating consultation on the best way to meet this concern, in line with the protocol agreed at the recent national bishops' meeting. At the same time the rights of women to be held as equal before God and in our nation are celebrated in the recent historic announcements. To know that the next Governor General of Australia will, for the first time, be a woman is momentous and a further redressing of the gender imbalance in our society.

Through the centuries of the Christian tradition two principles have been uncompromising: the individual's capacity to proclaim the Gospel and the ability to associate together in worship. Various principles and traditions have been adopted or lost but Christians have unwaveringly held that the right to proclaim the Gospel and the right to come together in worship are fundamental to our faith. Stephen, the first Christian Martyr, was put to death for asserting his right to make known the good news of Christ. Many have followed Stephen's path, who in turn was inspired by the death of Jesus on the cross. Let us not take lightly the religious freedoms we enjoy today in this country.

In a nation where we are free to believe in Christ as a matter of conscience and choice, the individual is free to choose to commit to a transformed life or not. Two exemplars of that choice were Archbishop Sir Frank Little and Archbishop Robert Dann, fine men whose humble and faithful service led their dioceses and inspired their people to that transformation in Christ. May our heartfelt prayers continue to be made on behalf of all in places where Christian observance means threats, fear, violence and even death. When next you make your way to your place of worship, take time to give thanks to Almighty God for the rights we enjoy, the freedom to travel openly to our parishes, to publicly teach and preach the Gospel of our Lord.

May 2008

Walking for Millennium Development Goals

Lambeth's 'Walk of Witness' through the streets of London was unforgettable, up to 1500 bishops, spouses and others, banner carrying and walking to urge governments to keep their promises to meet the Millennium Development Goals. Simple, effective faith in action. I invite you to join with me on 25 September for a day of prayer and fasting in solidarity with the people who live without any of the benefits of health or education or comfort that we enjoy. This is the day when the United Nations meets to discuss its commitment to the Millenium Development Goals.

'What good is it, my brothers and sisters, if people claim to have faith but have no deeds? Can such faith save them?' (James 2:14)

The letter from James is fresh in my mind as I write, having recently returned from the Australian Anglican Schools Network Conference where the theme was 'Faith in Action'. So too my AIM 4 Melbourne, Anglicans in mission in Geelong and Melbourne, faith in action and action for faith as we seek to bring to our communities the message of God's love for us through Jesus Christ incarnate. Fresh Connections 2009 is the implementation of AIM 4 Melbourne. I am grateful for the responses received to date from many of you who want to give yourself wholeheartedly to this expression of faith in action.

Last year, I commenced my engagement with the diocese, through visits to many parts of Melbourne and Geelong, reaching out to individuals where they are. Listening to people in shopping centres or to university students or manufacturing workers, their needs and anxieties emerged. Global warming or the stewardship of our fragile planet ... parents caring for adult children with disabilities ... the effects of our society on the young with the increasing incidence of depressive illnesses ... the care for our older generations ... the inequality of Indigenous and non Indigenous ... socioeconomic pressures and coping with more straitened circumstances... issues such as these occupy and even trouble the minds of those who live in the diocese.

Living in Australia, however, makes us comparatively fortunate, even rich, when we consider our sisters and brothers throughout the developing world. Our problems, though real, become less significant when we reflect on the millions for whom access to food, clean water, shelter, health care, education and employment cannot be relied upon.

Transactional is the word I have used to describe much of our way of life here. Material possessions measure our standard of living and we think in transactional ways. By way of example I cite the carbon trading emissions system announced by the government which must be acknowledged as a significant initiative through which to reduce the effects of carbon emissions on the planet. It is still a trading scheme, however, and transactional.

Relationships are the answer, first with God in Christ and then with each other, those who are our neighbours according to the Bible, whether here or in countries affected by our high standards of living. Let us accept the challenge and take the message of relationships to the community. With the lay people, clergy, area deans, archdeacons and bishops, will you join in our mission to the diocese and the community?

The values of our transactional, material driven society can change. Deep inside us, we know that financial and material security is not enough. I believe there is a hunger in people for such a change, a hunger for values which nurture and fulfil, a hunger to know the 'other' that is beyond humanity but has so wonderfully met us in Christ, the 'other' that is God. Will you walk with me, in the Year of Fresh Connections, when with intentional activities and events we call the people of our cities to the joy of knowing and relating to God? This can be our 'Walk of Witness' in the place where God has called us to live as disciples.

We are Anglicans together in mission in Melbourne and Geelong. May God's grace give us the energy, strength and wisdom to connect with each other and with our community, in the conviction of the risen Christ.

September 2008

True faith requires us to trust that all will be well

As you know, Joy and I were recently in Darwin with a group of younger Melbourne Anglicans. As it turned out, I needed to go to the Northern Land Council office in Darwin to pick up a permit to enable a visit to Minyerri and Gunbalanya. Walking from where I had parked I saw an elderly Aboriginal woman sitting outside one of Darwin's well known Art Galleries. She was a retired deaconess from Ngukurr who I had known well from my time there as the bishop. After our greeting I asked what she was doing. 'I'm waiting here to get a lift to Katherine', she said. 'Who is taking you?', I asked. It quickly transpired that there was nothing apparently organised so I offered to drive her down with my group, we had a spare seat. Later on, another dimension came out as she told the story to the gallery owner and others, 'The Holy Spirit told me to just to sit and wait and someone would come and give me a lift to Katherine.'

My friend had travelled 650 km from her home at Ngukurr with complete faith in the guidance of the Holy Spirit, knowing that she needed to go another 350 km to reach the Katherine Christian Convention. What an exemplar of faith, of trust in God who is freely accessible to all who would believe! Her destination and confidence in arrival were for her of uncomplicated clarity.

We are all on a journey. Journey as a metaphor for life is time honoured in literature. The concept of journey on which I am focused as I write, however, is that of the Diocese of Melbourne. Where are we going? As a diocese, our mission is clear, to 'go therefore and make disciples of all nations, baptising them in the name of the Father and of the Son and of the Holy Spirit, and teaching them to obey everything I have commanded you' (Matthew 28:19-20). I am convinced that this enduring purpose of the Church is poised to find and even more focused outcome in the Diocese of Melbourne. Celebrated for its diversity, the Diocese of Melbourne is strongly positioned to be a powerful force for the sharing of the Good News of Christ and of incorporation of believers into the life of the Church.

The May Budget Synod was an important stage in our current journey. A good debate of important issues but unanimous support for the way forward. In the planning leading up to the budget and on the day of Synod I was strongly conscious of the Holy Spirit leading us through and around all complications and impediments. The next stage of the journey is the strategic planning process which will integrate all aspects of the strategic work already happening – Fresh Connections, the Interim Ministry and Mission Commission, the governance and budget process ... – with previous strategic plans and the 2010 budget development, holding above all to our mission as Twenty First Century disciples of Jesus.

Compared with the open roads of the Northern Territory our own roads in Melbourne don't always seem to be so freely moving. I had a recent experience of this on the Monash Freeway on my way to an evening event at a parish. As the car inched its way forward – it was tempting to feel worried and frustrated. Should I have left earlier or taken a different route? But with no way out of the traffic jam except to go forward at a snail's pace, patience and acceptance were the only possible attitudes of mind that preserved spiritual peace. We often need to trust that all will eventually be well.

The journey of our diocese will meet many such obstacles even apparent times of slow movement but with a proper focus on our Lord and his gifts to us it will be a true journey of faith.

June 2009

Welcome must be more than 'hello' at the door

Welcoming the Stranger is a Godly precept. Anyone who is not 'us' can be the 'stranger'. Topical in Melbourne right now is the perception that we Victorians are not welcoming of overseas students. The pictures of some of the injured Indian students who have been assaulted are truly shocking and must be very distressing to their families and community overseas. Arguably the attacks have not been racist but instead, incidents of Melbourne's unacceptable level of violence. No matter what, it is appalling if any individual – citizen or tourist – is made to feel unsafe or unwelcome on our streets.

The streets of Melbourne surrounding the Anglican Centre are at any time of the day or night filled with people from a wide variety of ethnic backgrounds. Multicultural Melbourne is never more evident than in the environs of Flinders Street Station, Federation Square, the Meridian International Hotel School and St Paul's Cathedral. Non Indigenous Australians, welcomed to our country from places far away, can be proud of their individual ethnic ancestry as well as the collective heritage of Australians. '*For those who've come across the seas, We've boundless plains to share*', proclaims our National Anthem.

Multicultural Melbourne is also multifaith Melbourne and members of minority faith communities are an important part of our community, contributing to discussions about the shape of Australian society. We will have a unique opportunity to witness this microcosm of the world later this year when the Parliament of the World's Religions meets for the first time in Australia. Held every five years in a city of the globe, the Parliament is likely to bring 10,000 visitors to Victoria. With a multiplicity of events staged from 3 to 9 December, the Parliament will give Anglicans of the Diocese of Melbourne the opportunity of offering hospitality in the Cathedral, in our churches and in public places. We need to hold together the generosity of our hospitality to strangers and the clarity of our faith in Jesus Christ, as we seek to be in neighbourly relationship with people who follow the teachings of the world's religions. I encourage you to find out more or register to attend. The website is www.parliamentofreligions.org.

May we always be welcoming of strangers! More recently asylum seeker boats have provoked various responses, not all welcoming. We only have to look to the Letter to the Hebrews to read:

Be not forgetful to entertain strangers: for thereby some have entertained angels unawares.

It is my hope that those who genuinely seek refuge will find a home in Australia and peace. Our Sudanese, Karen and Tamil congregations are examples of welcoming people who have fled from conflict in their own countries. In fact, the emphasis on multicultural ministry generally is to ensure that all, irrespective of race or language, can find a place of welcome in God's church.

Most of us can be self-congratulatory in reviewing our own levels of hospitality offered to others, in simple friendliness or through inviting people to family meals, but how do we measure up in the parishes? I am certain that there is much good practice of hospitality in our churches.

As Archbishop, I am in the privileged position of not only being cordially and generously welcomed when I visit parishes but also of being warmly invited to services and other parish events. I have heard recently, however, of two contrary stories. One was of an Anglican who deliberately visited several churches, mostly finding that the seemingly friendly congregations were in fact only friendly amongst themselves. The other was of a member of the clergy who, soon after retirement and visiting a few parishes, was surprised to discover that there was little or no structure in place to make newcomers feel at home.

I fear that the reality of the welcome offered to strangers in our Anglican churches may fall short of the ideal and I challenge us all with the following questions. What happens to strangers who visit your church? Do you have people on duty to welcome anyone who is new? Is the welcome more than just a hello at the door? Are visitors looked after, particularly after the service, and introduced to others over a cup of tea? Whether or not they are shopping around for a church to join, do strangers go away from your parish feeling they have been properly greeted and valued in their time with you? Are they likely to have bridges built, so that their faith in Christ might be strengthened?

The disciples on the Emmaus road were welcoming of the Stranger, only to find that they were entertaining the Lord Jesus Christ. Let us be truly welcoming of strangers for thereby we, too, may entertain angels unawares.

August 2009

Deeper wisdom of faith could challenge knife violence

In the week of my writing these words, news emerged of a twelve-year-old schoolboy who had died from stab wounds after a schoolyard fight at a Brisbane school. I know the location of the school well as the suburb, Shorncliffe, is not far away from where I grew up and where I later ministered in a nearby parish. It is on a tranquil headland overlooking the waters of Moreton Bay, not far from the pier where the Brisbane to Gladstone Yacht race is started on Good Friday each year. Another schoolboy, a year older, remains in custody after the stabbing.

One young life brought to an abrupt end, another inevitably altered by the legal and psychological consequences of this action. Grieving family members and a whole school community left in shock and disbelief.

The fact that schoolchildren get into a fight is not exceptional but the carrying of a knife and its use in such a dispute is disturbing, to say the least. In a society that is awash with violent depictions of conflictual behaviour, it might also be unexceptional that for some young people this influences how they behave. Violent video games, violent movies and the growing reality of knife-related violence between adults is not easily firewalled from the influences that shape the thinking and value judgments of young lives. The shallow masculinity of popular culture is easily normalised as the example to which young boys entering adolescence aspire.

Many of us were hopeful when the gun buyback scheme was implemented in Australia after the tragic events at Port Arthur, Tasmania on 28 April 1996. It was a small loss of freedom for some, but well worth it to live in a society that would have less access to firearms.

Undoubtedly the question will be asked: has the time come now to restrict access to knives? It sounds almost impossible given their usefulness and ubiquity but in a society usually unwilling to confront the connection between the sort of society we live in and its influence on young people, it is certain to be put forward as a solution.

But it is in better understanding the impact of societal patterns and role modelling on young people that there will be more fertile grounds for conversation. As a society we are unwilling to restrict the choices adults make as if that is of no consequence to others, notably children. I imagine that most people who play violent video games or watch violent movies have no risk of becoming violent themselves. They are able to distinguish reality from fantasy. It is less clear that this distinction is as easily made during earlier developmental stages.

It would be wrong to think that that we are encountering new questions that have not been answered before. The deeper wisdom of our faith tradition is a good place to look in confronting our present circumstances, whether they be the growing knife culture or the violence on our streets in Melbourne and Geelong. Young people are struggling to work out their identity in the face of violent role models. Boundaries for adults are blurred, the difference between right and wrong being less well defined. The life of Jesus is the ultimate role model for old and young. It is our distinctive vocation as Christians to affirm the knowledge of our Lord's life and teaching to the future of our community.

The future shape of our society is being molded in the lives of the young before our eyes. May we contribute to their choices by showing our Christian community as the place where these deeper truths are lived.

March 2010

Perfect love casts out fear

I am always interested in the culture in which I live. I started ordained ministry in a cross-cultural context and have lived in a number of different cultural settings. This helps me to understand both the dominant influence of culture but also the relative nature of culture when contrasted with realities that ultimately are more real. Culture shapes our thinking and our behaviour but does not fully define us. Culture may be understood in terms that honour the past or value just the present, as well as the mix of positions in between.

The culture of non-Indigenous Australians, what we mostly experience as Australian culture, has a long history of insecurity and anxiety as defining qualities of 'who we are'. For the first non-Indigenous Australians there was anxiety about their survival and the success of their invasion of Indigenous lands. Churches in our diocese contain memorials to settlers who died from being speared in frontier conflicts. The Depression of the 1890's, the anxiety about invasion by Russian Fleets at the beginning of the 20th century, the Depression of the 1930s, the fear of Japanese invasion in the second World War, Cold War anxieties from the time of the Korean War onwards – the list goes on.

What interests me is how we assess risk and frame our concern. It is arguable that the people of our world are in less risk from a nuclear war than we were in the 1960's. Certainly the anxiety about nuclear war was higher then than now. Familiarity with circumstances habituates us to them and dulls our sense of alarm compared with when something first comes to our attention. Unless experience confirms the earlier perception of risk there is a trend towards ignoring it and just 'getting on with life'. We see this in planning decisions that have been made to allow houses to be built in flood or fire prone areas. The knowledge of risk is there but as the experience of the occurrence recedes, it reaches a point where the concern is allayed. The majority act as if it will never re-occur and are not prone to anxiety about that likelihood.

But still anxiety remains. No matter how much some things drop out of our awareness others quickly take their place. I often wonder if we have a culture of anxiety that risks defining our views about life and our life in the church. The words of 1 John 4:18, 'There is no fear in love, but perfect love casts our fear; for fear has to do with punishment, and whoever fears has not reached perfection in love' must be some of the most challenging for Christians and how we live.

If I am right about Australian culture it would follow that Christians will often find ourselves at odds with our culture, even if it is only on this point. I sometimes hear the language of fear used within the church, about its future or present effectiveness. In my consultations about vision and directions, the appreciation of all that is happening has been encouraging but I also have picked up on negative thinking about the health of the diocese and the church. Those with an anxious outlook may have heard only part of a story or may be affected by a situation in their own parish. We are of course all entitled to have our moments of feeling dismayed. But Christians are people of hope and with God's grace our future is assured. We are given the strategies and skills to welcome people into our local churches and to undertake outreach to the community. It is my hope that the way we come together as Anglicans in mission in Melbourne and Geelong will enrich and connect us within the church and its culture, as well as into the community, and make a transforming contribution back into the Australian culture.

June 2010

'Comfort them, Lord, in this disaster'

The following is Archbishop Philip Freier's sermon given at a special Eucharist with prayers for the people of Christchurch New Zealand on 24 February in St Paul's Cathedral Melbourne.

The tragic circumstances of the devastating earthquake in Christchurch, New Zealand confront us with a reality beyond our imaginations. Think of a building like this or any of the iconic structures in Melbourne and contemplate them lying in ruins – it defies our sense of what is possible. Imagine those who are trapped in rubble and their dark and lonely ordeal, perhaps hearing a distant sound – a hope raised – but still the dark and cold – how can we who have not experienced it take it in? It is precisely because these events depict a reality that is beyond our imagining that we must come before God in prayer and painful recognition at our smallness in the face of such forces.

The overwhelming power of these forces of nature readily convinced the people of antiquity and perhaps some in our own day that these must be the forces of an angry divinity, God's revenge on an unfaithful world:

Then the earth reeled
and rocked;
the foundations of the heavens trembled
and quaked, because [God] was angry (2 Samuel 22:8).

Geological science shows us that the earthquake responsible for the destruction that has happened in Christchurch has indeed the same source as the forces which built the mountains in the ancient millennia of geological time – the forces of creation still at work in the world today – the forces that make our human engineering skill look puny when they are unleashed in such power. As much as we marvel at the New Zealand Alps for their height and snow-covered grandeur they are physical witnesses to the sometimes slow and silent intersection of tectonic plates that occasionally release cataclysmic energy when pressured geological strata suddenly fracture under the buildup of such enormous pressure.

One thing we know in these times of natural disaster, and we have learned it here in Australia through fire, wind and flood – is the vulnerability of our expectations that what we have around us is stable and sure to continue like it is into the future. No one can live with the constant anxiety of disaster waiting for them at every turn – we must live in a high degree of confidence about the future, but this is why such events always catch us by surprise.

We gather to pray for the people who we know personally who are missing, for the families who fear the worst or have had the death of their loved ones confirmed. We pray for strength for those who are trapped, that God would be with them to ease their fear and give them the courage to endure until their rescue arrives. We pray for emergency workers along with the ordinary people who are doing extraordinary jobs; people who have set their determination to rescue people and restore essential services, especially as fatigue sets in, and the trauma of what they have experienced saps energy within tiring bodies.

Each of us will come today with a personal experience, visual image, mental fear or whatever it is that compels you to join here today. Be confident that in this holy place God receives those prayers and hears the thoughts of your mind and sees the images that have been seared in your brain. If you can do nothing else, sit in the presence of God with those things that are too heavy to bear on your own.

As the Psalmist prayed: You have caused the land to quake; you have torn it open; repair the cracks in it, for it is tottering (Psalm 60:2). In a world that has literally 'fallen apart' we join in solidarity with the people of New Zealand, coming with nothing but our empathy – our fears – and our shared awareness of vulnerability. In prayer we make ourselves vulnerable to God who through Jesus Christ has revealed our true destiny as sons and daughters of God – a destiny that is not just defined by our weakness in the face of nature's forces but is confidently secure in God no matter what. Psalm 46.2 puts this well: Therefore we will not fear, though the earth should change, though the mountains shake in the heart of the sea. I would like to conclude with this version of Diana Macalintal's prayer after the Haiti earthquake:

Lord, at times such as this,
when we realise that the ground beneath our feet
is not as solid as we had imagined, we plead for your mercy.
As the things we have built crumble about us,
we know too well how small we truly are -
Do not forget us now.
Today, so many people are afraid. They wait in fear of the next tremor.
They hear the cries of the injured amid the rubble.
They roam the streets in shock at what they see.
And they fill the air with wails of grief
and the names of missing dead. Comfort them, Lord, in this disaster.
Be their rock when the earth refuses to stand still,
and shelter them under your wings when homes no longer exist.
Pierce, too, our hearts with compassion,
we who watch from afar,
Move us to act swiftly this day, and to pray unceasingly for those without hope.

And once the shaking has ceased, the images of destruction have stopped filling the news,
and our thoughts return to life's daily rumblings,
let us not forget that we are all your children
and they, our brothers and sisters.
We are all the work of your hands.
For though the mountains leave their place and the hills be tossed to the ground,
your love shall never leave us, and your promise of peace will never be shaken.
Amen

March 2011

Valuing Indigenous knowledge in contemporary society

A few weeks ago I travelled to Galiwin'ku in North East Arnhem Land for a week of leave and family reunion. This is not a place that I had visited before even though I had known something about it from my earlier associations in teaching in the north during the 1970s and more recently when I lived in Darwin. The flight to Galiwin'ku was a comfortable one on a modern turbo-prop aircraft, a far cry from the earlier days when this former Methodist mission was serviced by ship from Darwin and by a light aircraft flown by the missionary Harold Shepperdson or 'Bapa Sheppie' as he was known. The Elcho Island mission at Galiwin'ku was founded in 1942 from the nearby Milingimbi Mission. Shepperdson's commitment to flying was the means through which he kept contact with people living on their clan estates and is a factor in the flourishing of the outstation movement in that vicinity.

One way to understand the social organisation of Indigenous Australia is to see clan groups as a primary locus of identity, these clans existing within and sometimes across language groups. Such a pattern of social organisation has necessitated the development of sophisticated patterns of peacemaking and reconciliation to resolve tension. Some of these have been recommended as instruments of Indigenous and non-Indigenous reconciliation, the Makarrata movement in the 1980's for example arose out of insights from the Makarrata ceremony of Groote Eylandt and south eastern Arnhem Land. I was able recently while on Elcho Island in North Eastern Arnhem Land to coincide with the Mawul Rom ceremony.

The Rev'd Dr Djiniyini Gondarra has been the person to open this peace making ceremony to a wider participation that sees many non-Indigenous people participate in Mawul Rom as part of a Masters degree in Indigenous knowledge from Charles Darwin University in the Northern Territory. The Mawul Rom project seeks to 'engage people in an exploration of the similarities and differences of approach; in decision making and dispute resolution; between Indigenous and non-Indigenous cultural spheres.' There may be other examples that could be cited alongside this significant initiative in valuing Indigenous knowledge and applying its insights to contemporary society.

In 1973, the Australian Board of Missions chairman at the time, John Munro, reflected on the missed opportunities of Anglican mission amongst Australian Aborigines. 'I, personally, think it sad indeed that a people whose indigenous cultic practices contained so much which would have adapted easily to a healthy sacramentalism, e.g. the Churinga, the topography's identification with the dream-time, the totemistic elements in the social order, etc., should for the most part have come to know the cultic side of Christianity in only one of many ways. But all that is a story of lost chances.'

It could be now that these 'lost chances' were not truly lost but have found a place through the Aboriginal Christians in Arnhem Land offering the treasures 'old and new' from within their culture and their faith.

August 2011

The power of a constitutional framework for the national church

On 1 January this year, the 50th anniversary of the operation of the Constitution of the Anglican Church of Australia occurred. Until our constitution was agreed there was a long period of not having the constitutional framework to make the national church as much of a reality as it has been over the past half century. Strangely enough the anniversary has gone by with barely a mention. Even though it was long in the making, this constitution has provided us with the framework to be a national church and to take our place as an autonomous province of the worldwide Anglican Communion.

I'm not sure whether it is the tension in the worldwide communion or just a cultural propensity to play down our achievements that has meant this fiftieth anniversary has gone unacknowledged. In earlier international discussions the example of the Anglican Church of Australia and its constitutional underpinnings has been promoted as a model of how different expressions of Anglicanism can cohere together in missional and Christian unity. It sounds ironic doesn't it? Commending our experience internationally but coy about celebrating it at home.

Like many in our Church, I have not known of any other Anglican Church. Despite the endurance of 'Church of England' in popular memory, most of us have only known what it is like to be part of the Anglican Church of Australia. To make the national constitution the clear authority outside of the Diocese each of the Provinces (approximating states in the Federation of the Commonwealth) have let their capacity for making legislation become inactive. This has been a significant compromise that would have surprised our predecessors in Colonial Australia who did not see that a united vision for Australia would prevail.

So, for instance, the Clergy of Melbourne Diocese celebrated the 25th Anniversary of Charles Perry's episcopate by signing a testimonial to him on St Peter's Day, 1872. Along with recalling his many achievements they looked forward to the further development of the church. 'And we earnestly desire that Your Lordship may live to see an extension of the episcopate in the Colony, feeling as we do that our organisation will be incomplete until the see of Melbourne occupies a metropolitan position in a sub-divided province.'

My experience may be unique, but from the perspective of ministering in the Diocese of Carpentaria and the Diocese of the Northern Territory it is clear to me that we need a national church with keen mutual concern so as to ensure ministry to all parts of our nation. The late Canon Fred Bedbrook, who led my ordination retreat on Thursday Island, was someone whose vision for and contribution to the national church was inspiring. His advocacy for the National Home Mission Fund gave a confidence that we were not forgotten, in our isolated places of service and that the parishes of the capital cities stood with us in our task. I believe that there is much that we can continue to do together as a national church even though we are bound to regard the individual dioceses as the fundamental locus of mission and resource.

May 2012

Lessons learned in a life of radical commitment to holiness

What a joy it is to look forward to the celebration of our Lord's birth. The season of Advent properly calls us to a time of spiritual preparation, a time of penitence and fasting so that we can better focus on God rather than ourselves.

In the early days of my ministry as the priest at Kowanyama, I spent some time in Cairns with a retired missionary teacher, Sylvia Card, to learn about her life at Kowanyama when it was still known as Mitchell River Mission. I spoke to her about her life as a missionary and how she had come to spend her working life in that remote part of far north Queensland. She told me that she was one of Father Maynard's 'penitents' and how she was inspired to offer her life for missionary service through the formation of her faith in Melbourne, specifically at St Peter's Eastern Hill. Known as Sister Maud when she was in Melbourne, Sylvia Card was for most of the time the only qualified teacher at the Mission School. Arising from her Catholic spirituality, her motto for the school children was 'Work hard, Play hard, Pray hard'. In that distant place, far from Melbourne, she worked to live out her profession as a Christian and as an Anglican who embraced Catholic spirituality.

Matthew 16:15-17 *He said to them, 'But who do you say that I am?' Simon Peter answered, 'You are the Messiah, the Son of the living God.' And Jesus answered him, 'Blessed are you, Simon son of Jonah! For flesh and blood has not revealed this to you, but my Father in heaven.*

Sylvia Card's life was the intensely personal response to the same question that Jesus posed to Peter, '...who do you say that I am?' Like Peter, Sylvia and all who are faithful Christians answer, 'You are the Messiah, the Son of the living God.' This is the primary confession we make, that Jesus is Lord, and in those words recognise that through Jesus Christ it has not just become possible but has become a reality for us to enter into a relationship of love with the living God.

Sylvia Card's response was also deeply personal, a radical commitment to holiness and commitment to the worship of god in the liturgical rites of the church. I think this is demonstrated in these words she wrote advertising the Christmas worship at Mitchell River in 1967:

> Christmass confessions
> Please come to prepare for Christmass.
> At Christmass God was born to save us from our sins.
> The Blessed Virgin Mother held God in her arms.
> At Confession, God cleanses us so that we may hold God
> in our hearts at Holy Communion.

Her spirituality with its commitment to personal holiness of life and radical commitment to being sent to proclaim the gospel. For us we can desire no greater calling than to follow our Lord in our daily lives earnestly seeking the continuation of that transformation that is Christ's gift to us, as the new humanity he has come to gather to himself, the one true shepherd.

November 2012

God's abiding love remains a haven against violence

It is a while since I visited Egypt back in January 2008, a time that coincided with the Orthodox Christmas. I visited St Mark's Cathedral in Cairo on the Coptic Christmas Eve. It was not just because the time of year naturally drew attention to the infancy narratives about Jesus, but the verse from Matthew's Gospel (Matthew 2:15) that recalls Hosea 11:1 was very present in the telling of the story of identity of the Egyptian Church: 'Out of Egypt I have called my son.'

That Egypt had been the safe haven for the Holy Family and thus an integral part of the divine plan of salvation's fulfilment was not lost on the Egyptian Christians as they, even then, hung onto a precarious minority position in Egyptian society.

That was in the Mubarak era and much has changed since then, some for the worse. The civil war in Syria added to the sustained hostility to Christians in Iraq. The list goes on and confronts us with the reality that Christians are finding their part in these places increasingly uncertain. We forget at our folly that such lands are the cradle of ancient Christianity. It would be an appalling instance of naivety or, worse, chauvinism for us to be blind to the sufferings of contemporary Middle Eastern Christians. After all, is it not the case that the faith we have received has come to us through faithful witnesses who endured similar sufferings?

It will come as no surprise that times of Christian celebration also provide opportunities for the fanatical opponents of Christianity to throw their worst hostility at Christians and their places of worship particularly. Pray that the Christians in Egypt, the Middle

East, Pakistan, Nigeria and Sudan – to name just a few – might be preserved in safety this Christmas. Remember them too before God in your own celebrations. After all, what we do in such confidence and safety is all that they are seeking.

The experience of the Holy Family also alerts us to the long story of suffering for many millions of displaced people in the world. We know a little of this from the enormous attention that boat arriving asylum seekers receive in our country. Those who received Joseph and Mary and their infant son with generosity could not have imagined what part they were playing in God's purposes. We thank God for them and their compassion. Likewise we do not know how God can work in the lives of people when they are treated with generosity and kindness.

I feel privileged to meet many people for whom that has been their experience of Australia. It might not look like that if we were just to focus on the policies reckoned to deter boat arrivals, but the deep decency and compassion some experience is transformative for those traumatised by war and displacement from their homelands. Some are so transformed by this compassion, especially when it is given in Christ's name, that they seek unity with the source of this blessing in baptism. Give thanks for those amongst our Church who have made this journey and found their place amongst us.

December 2013

Australia's Indigenous and non-Indigenous – equal in God's eyes

Reconciliation is a key strand of our diocesan vision and directions for 2014-16. We have recently celebrated National Reconciliation Week which is bookmarked by the dates of the 27 May commemoration of the 1967 referendum and the 3 June 1992 Mabo decision. We now have a third key date. In 2008, I gave a talk to The Melbourne University Graduate Union on 'After sorry what next?' It had been on 13 February that year when many listened intently to the 'Sorry', the statement of apology to Australia's Aboriginal Peoples given in Parliament by Prime Minister Kevin Rudd.

As I stood in Federation Square watching the big screen to see and hear the Prime Minister speak those words, I felt a sense of history in the making. The atmosphere was emotional with so many people linked together by a shared expectation and sincerity of feeling. For a long time, there had been a desire for such words to be spoken with sincerity by the national leader, words spoken in many contexts elsewhere, state parliaments and Anglican Church Synods to name but a couple.

I was reminded of that other powerful occasion which had seemed to set a fresh course for our nation – the 1967 referendum through which Aboriginal people were able to be counted in the Census and the Commonwealth was given a role in Indigenous matters. My point was that we have often reached watershed moments when there has been a powerful sense of putting a past wrong to right, the 1967 referendum, Paul Keating's 'Redfern' speech in 1992 and Rudd's Stolen generation apology in 2008 surely number amongst them.

These were powerful symbols of a resolve to shape a different future. Symbolism alone, however, proves never to be enough. Symbolism is an important action but insufficiently substantial by itself. This is the reason we in the diocese are impelled to action through the development of a Reconciliation Action Plan or RAP. We are close to writing up our Reflect RAP, the first stage of the action plans recommended by Reconciliation Australia.

The statistics of Aboriginal and Torres Strait Islander life expectancy and measures of health and education are important and we must close the gap so that opportunity is equally available. But statistics do not actually move people to engagement in the shared humanity that we have. I am eager that we find that place where our aspirations as Indigenous and non-Indigenous people meet, as people in Australia sharing the same humanity, having similar aspirations and goals, coming to an understanding of the way we can move forward together.

We must tell the story of a nation of Indigenous and non-Indigenous, equal in God's eyes and the laws of our nation but different in heritage and culture, together in one nation, equally accessing good standards of education and health, contributing to our society, contributing to a rich culture that is a mix of ancient and new. A story of achievement, of mutual respect, of valuing those Aboriginal ways of living and relating that have held good through time.

June 2014

The new Primate calls for fervent prayer

I am grateful to all who have kindly sent me greetings of encouragement for my role as Primate of Australia. This role is of course additional to my primary role as Archbishop to Melbourne and I intend to devise plans over the next few months to enable this new responsibility to be added smoothly to current operations. We are in an exciting time in the life of the Melbourne Diocese as we work through making our diocese 'mission shaped'. It is a good time to add the primacy into these considerations.

The brief visit of the Archbishop of Canterbury was also a source of encouragement for the many that were able to be present in the Cathedral for my inauguration service. I was impressed in my private meetings with Archbishop Justin Welby that he has a clarity about what he hopes to achieve in his term in that important position. It is well known that there are tensions in the international communion which will take great acts of grace and forgiveness to come back to the kind of Christian relationships proper to a Communion. I am happy to support Archbishop Justin in his efforts and I share his vision.

The inauguration service emphasised the power of corporate worship. I understand that there were about 1,500 people present in St Paul's and all to whom I spoke appreciated the solidarity and sharing of purpose that we celebrated. We are so fortunate to be able to gather in the many churches of our diocese as we worship God and give thanks for all that has been done for us and for our salvation in our Lord Jesus Christ. What a contrast to the situation of Christians in those other parts of the world where they are hunted away from their communities, where they have lost their lives and livelihoods and have had their churches closed.

I am sure that we are all overwhelmed by the fast-changing events in the world. Our individual human capacity to hold these things in our minds is limited. We too quickly move on from the miserable situation of the Christian girls abducted from their school in Northern Nigeria to the horrors of Northern Iraq, without necessarily being aware of the many other situations. We are sure to feel that these tragedies exceed our human wisdom. That is the reason Christians need to be fervent in prayer for these many in their afflictions. We have a solidarity with each other in our sufferings through our common membership of the Christian Church. It is simply impossible for us not to feel the pain of those other members of the body of Christ and then to speak and act in response to their need.

This scale of world events as they impact upon our fellow Christians gives an immediacy to the words of Luke 14:27: '*Whoever does not carry the cross and follow me cannot be my disciple*'. May our discipleship be deepened by the witness of those in these hard places.

September 2014

An ordered society, evidence of God's hand

Whatever might be said about the 20th Century it was a period where it seemed apparent that the world had been divided up amongst different nation states. Some of these states certainly fought destructive wars against each other and state boundaries were enlarged or reduced depending on the outcome of the conflict but by and large there was an apparent commitment to maintaining the integrity of nation states and ensuring their continuity notwithstanding these horrific events. Throughout the century most of the colonies established in the centuries before were brought into the community of nations as independent equal members.

What has emerged in the first fifteen years of our present century is the increasing reality of 'ungoverned spaces' often within the asserted boundaries of otherwise recognised nation states. It is well known that large areas of Iraq and Syria are in this situation, but the reality of such 'ungoverned spaces' occurs on several continents. We are fortunate to live on a continent where government authority is strong and where there is a robust legal basis to balance this authority and our individual rights.

With the growth of these 'ungoverned spaces' I have been interested to look at the biblical evidence as it concerns the corporate identity of people. Certainly the existence of different nations is understood as being as ancient as the dispersion that follows from God's destruction of the Tower of Babel. Indeed Deuteronomy 32:8 speaks of the identity and boundaries of nations as divinely ordered, 'When the Most High apportioned the nations, when he divided humankind, he fixed the boundaries of the peoples according to the number of the gods; the LORD's own portion was his people, Jacob his allotted share.'

Acts 17: 26, 27 essentially reiterates this understanding but ties the differentiation of peoples amongst the nations to their search for God, a search that is answered in Christ. As Acts 17 quotes St Paul in Athens it is easy to see his teaching being received by people familiar with the story of the destruction of the Tower of Babel as being about God's generous healing of human division in Christ. The teaching of St Paul in the epistles sees the distinction between peoples on the basis of language, ethnicity or culture as at best provisional or secondary to the unity that is possible in Christ. Paul himself is unhesitating in appealing to the order of the Roman Empire and the privileges his status as a Roman citizen conferred when his rights were abused.

The teaching of the New Testament maintains the assertion of God as the true source of earthly power with Romans 13 being a crisp statement of that position. Here an organised system of authority is clearly envisaged not the chaos of brigandry or 'ungoverned spaces.' The orderly character of human society is the sign of God's hand in human affairs. Order is better than chaos. Just look at the rush of people out of these 'ungoverned spaces' seeking to find refuge in ordered societies. As people find their reconciliation with God in Christ and with each other we should look for the reign of peace to increase in the world. I think that this makes our proclamation of the Gospel – especially to the least responsive people and most unreceptive people groups all the more urgent.

September 2015

The gift of seeing criticism as divine blessing

In a world where certainty of opinions is valued more than the capacity to admit error, an ancient story in 2 Samuel 16 is a good point of focus for our own reflections on power. The story is a simple one and is an incident that occurs on David's flight from Jerusalem to the region across the Jordan river. Before his party reaches the Jordan they are confronted by a man named Shimei, a distant relative of David. Shimei denounces David as a 'man of blood' and hurls curses and abuse across a small valley as David passes. This phrase, 'man of blood', carries the sense that David has 'blood on his hands' and is guilty of the death of innocent people. Naturally enough the more adventurous and indignant in David's band want to cross the valley and kill Shimei for insulting their leader.

This is all natural enough and is part of the drama of human interactions which is re-enacted, even if not to the point of such a drastic intention, by countless people across the world each day. Our capacity to pull together with the people to whom we owe loyalty at times of threat is all too obvious in many situations of life. So too is our capacity to strike out against criticism. What is remarkable in the 2 Samuel story is David's restraint. He holds back Abishai who is determined to strike down Shimei and recognises that God is speaking a truth to him through these unwelcome words. 'Let him alone and let him curse', David says, 'for the LORD has bidden him'.

David even hopes that these words of humiliation will eventually be in God's timing an occasion for blessing: 'It may be that the LORD will look on my distress, and the LORD will repay me with good for this cursing of me today.' It is not hard to see David's response to this situation as a precursor of St Paul's teaching in Romans 5:3-5 about the journey from suffering through to hope that is possible for those who know God's love. David recognises the moral weakness of his position even though he is in the physically stronger position over Shimei even to the point of unleashing Abishai's fury on him. David's recognition and restraint takes real character to do this and that character is certainly built on the foundation of knowing God and the divine love.

There is much that our world could learn from this story. Certainly, there is much that we can learn personally about the 'gift' that criticism can be in shaping the development of our character and being part of our own journey to hope through the struggles of life. It also carries a message for the Church to be able to learn from those who criticise, even if it is painful or even unfair. As David found there is truth in the words of others, and it is how we receive them and the attitude with which we reflect on them that makes the difference.

November 2015

Bombs can never destroy Christ's love for us

Easter 2016 was bookended by the terrorist attacks in Brussels and Lahore, the second apparently targeted at Christian families enjoying the Easter festivities.

Psalm 55 gives a perspective on how our human response to such events can be framed in God's wisdom and purposes. Verses 4 and 5 read, 'My heart is in anguish within me, the terrors of death have fallen upon me. Fear and trembling come upon me, and horror overwhelms me.'

We can be thankful to God that we have the empathy and ordinary decency to react immediately to such events with a depth of personal response. This response may range from outrage to sorrow and fear. I expect that we are all touched within ourselves by fear, this is natural as we extrapolate from what we have seen to our own circumstances and context. Our response is one of flight and the attempt to find a place of safety where such events can't reach us. We hope for anything to disrupt the direction of violence that seems to be gathering around us: 'Confuse, O Lord, confound their speech; for I see violence and strife in the city' (verse 9).

Whether it is in grainy security footage after such terrorist events or in the profiles of suicide bombers and terrorists released after such atrocities, I have been amazed how often beforehand they seemed to be people who just blended in to the society in which they lived. 'It is not my enemies who taunt me – I could bear that... But it is you, my equal, my companion, my familiar friend with whom I kept pleasant company' (verses 12, 13).

Undoubtedly we feel betrayed by anyone who turns their efforts to destruction rather than building up the common good. We need to know, however, that the offence of such acts of terror is not just measured in this world but is the subject of God's judgment.

The psalmist is confident of this and the theological realities of God's judgment and salvation apply as we look at who are in fact the damned in the aftermath of terrorist attacks. The psalmist models the response we need make, in prayer to God: 'I will call upon God, and the LORD will save me. Evening and morning and at noon I utter my complaint and moan, and he will hear my voice' (verse 17). Even in the worst of times when we are most distressed the reliability of God's love calls us to prayer and confidence in God.

The psalmist draws this reflection to a close with a very powerful assertion: 'Cast your burden on the LORD, and he will sustain you; he will never permit the righteous to be moved' (verse 22). That is to say that our salvation and God's personal love for us in Christ cannot be broken no matter what others do. Our mortal lives may be seized from us but our eternal standing in the love of God is secure. Our deepest response to both external events and our hearts' fears are summed up in the closing verse of the psalm: 'I will trust in you.' Keep this as your prayer to the Father who has revealed the depth of his love for us in the Son.

April 2016

'Such love, filling my emptiness... O Jesus, such love'

I have recently read a small book that concludes by positing some big questions about the mission of the Church in the present-day world. Interestingly enough, it is based on a lecture series given by Robert Jenson an American Lutheran theologian. His 'Theology in outline; Can these bones live?' starts off, as the title suggests, with the question posed in Ezekiel 37:3 to the prophet Ezekiel, 'Son of man, can these bones live?' Originally a question to Israel, Jenson argues that this is always the question for the Church and any assertions it makes about the way the world is. Are the things that concern the Church living realities or just a superstructure of language and practice that are no longer living or life giving?

On the way through his book he gives a highly effective summary of the main points of theology but for the purpose of my comments here I want to pick up on his closing remarks on the challenge of what he calls the 'nihilism' of contemporary western culture. This is a position that holds life is essentially empty and, because it is, demands all of the moments of waking to be filled by things and entertainment to conceal how confronting this emptiness actually is. Jenson sees this nihilism at work in a range of post-modern approaches. Such approaches tend towards suspicion of any assertions that life can be full and future focused, of any approaches that contradict the essential emptiness of life.

Plainly enough, Christianity posits a very different view of the world, a view that the world is created by God and should be received as gift, that God has acted decisively in the person of Jesus, the Son of God to bring humans into a new relationship with the divine and, most powerfully, that through Christ our future is with God in the new creation. Even one of these things upsets the view of the essential 'nothingness' of life and taken together with the other doctrines of Christianity propose a purposeful life for believers in a world that is not inevitably lost to chaos and destruction.

Jenson argues that for Christians to live their discipleship and for the Church to fulfill Christ's mission in this context we must return to the roots of our faith and live Christianity according to its own terms not according to the society's version of it. I don't think that he is being simply nostalgic about a world of antiquity that we can only enter by imagination but is describing what it means to live and communicate the faith in a world where the society around us no longer carries the faith in its structures and rhythms. It is no surprise that similar expressions of faith – like monasticism – are stirring modern Christians as they did the people of those first Christian centuries.

Look for the signs of the kingdom of 'nothingness' around you and confront it with those most ancient (and modern) truths of our faith that our Lord entrusted to his disciples. Live the Christian faith with passion and commitment. In the words of the Graham Kendrick song, 'Such love, filling my emptiness, such love, showing me holiness. O Jesus, such love'.

June 2016

We must own our past – both good and bad

During July, I participated in a significant event in the life of the Anglican Church of Australia: the seventieth anniversary of the founding of St Mary's Hostel in Alice Springs.

St Mary's was founded through the vision of Ken Leslie, Rector of Alice Springs at the time (later Chaplain at Timbertop and then Bishop of Bathurst) and the energies of Deaconess Eileen Heath. It is a place where the race politics of Australia and particularly Central Australia have been lived out in the lives of several generations of Aboriginal people. The founders of St Mary's acted out of a concern that children who had dual Aboriginal and non-Aboriginal heritage had very limited opportunities for education. Children were sent by their parents from cattle stations and towns all around the Northern Territory to live at St Mary's and attend the local government school.

Like many church ventures of this kind the efforts were poorly resourced and struggled to maintain and develop the kind of resources and staffing that were worthy of the founders' vision. The early success of St Mary's led to its appropriation as part of Government policy at the time of wrongfully removing children from their families – the painful experience of the Stolen Generations that remains raw for many who attended the seventieth anniversary event in July.

I took the opportunity to reiterate the statement of the Synod of the Diocese of the Northern Territory in 1997: 'This Synod recognises the pain and suffering endured by Aboriginal people forcibly removed from their families and apologises for any of our Church policies and actions that have ever contributed, in any way, to that hurt.'

I was able to speak as Primate of the Anglican Church of Australia owning the responsibility of the Church for all of our history, the true history, in both its positive and negative impacts. It is in this way, by truth telling, that we learn together and can find ways of celebrating the good and continuing to right the harm of the wrong. St John's Gospel is very clear about the liberating power of truth, in fact John 8:32, 'The truth will set you free', is the motto of the Anglican Communion.

I was impressed to see the courage of the former residents who have a special bond through their experience of being 'St Mary's kids' as well as the dedication of former staff members who have continued to live in Alice Springs.

Our Christian faith acknowledges that, in life, the good and the bad are often mixed together. Our faith calls us to look to a future where the pain of this life is gathered into the sufferings of Christ and transformed through his resurrection. Healing and wholeness await us in the future and breaks in on our present, as we accompany our blessed Saviour through life as his disciples.

On the way to that future, we have the blessing of knowing the encouragement of the good and the beautiful as signs of that future. May you be blessed on the journey of discipleship and know our Lord's healing presence in your life.

August 2016

The need for constitutional recognition

On 26 October, the Australian Government gave its response to the Referendum Council's report on Constitutional Recognition. Significantly it rejected the proposal that a 'Voice to Parliament' be constitutionally provided for as proposed by the 'Uluru Statement from the Heart'. There is a great risk that the importance of the Government's decision will be lost in the noise of the other political issues as we approach these last months of 2017. It may be helpful to repeat those things that I spoke about on the matter of Constitutional Recognition of Australia's First Nations People at the 2016 Synod. We had learned in August of that year that the proposed referendum on constitutional recognition of Indigenous Australians that had been scheduled for May 2017 was not going to proceed, with sometime in 2018 being then proposed as the earliest likely date.

With the Government's rejection of the Referendum Council's proposal, settling a proposition for a Referendum question seems even more distant. I hope that this does not signify a reduction of commitment to bring this opportunity for important change before the Australian people. There has been a long history of this issue being deferred. You may recall that at the 1999 referendum two questions were considered and both were rejected by the electorate, one was the republic question, the other was to alter the Constitution of the Commonwealth to insert a preamble.

Amongst other things the proposed preamble included the words, 'Honouring Aborigines and Torres Strait Islanders, the nation's first people, for their deep kinship with their lands and for the ancient and continuing cultures which enrich the life of our country'. This proposal to insert a preamble gained only

39% support across the country. In the negotiations following the inconclusive election of 2010, Prime Minister Julia Gillard promised a referendum on constitutional recognition for Indigenous people before the 2013 election. This did not take place and when it came to the 2013 election the successful candidate for Prime Minister, Tony Abbott had taken to the election the commitment to release a draft proposal for constitutional change within a year of taking office, but once again the matters became bogged down and did not proceed. Further dates that received earlier political support, when proposed, soon passed, especially the highly symbolic date of 27 May 2017, the 50th anniversary of the 1967 referendum that gave the Commonwealth powers to make laws that were specific to Aboriginal and Torres Strait Islander people.

Back in October 2016, I said, 'In my view it is highly likely that Aboriginal and Torres Strait Islander people will want any constitutional change to confer on the Commonwealth treaty making powers with the First Nations people of Australia. This will be controversial and will need strong bipartisan commitment between government and opposition parties to gain the public's confidence.'

We need to do all we can to encourage our politicians to unite around the cause for constitutional recognition of Aboriginal and Torres Strait Islander people. It is an important reform that cannot be allowed to drift indefinitely. It is a reform that also needs the highest confidence of Aboriginal and Torres Strait Islander people to succeed.

November 2017

Wailing, grief and hope as a life is remembered

I unexpectedly spent Ash Wednesday in Kowanyama, a remote Aboriginal community in far north Queensland. Unexpectedly, because I had been called at short notice to officiate at the funeral of a close member of the family that I had been adopted into many years ago when Joy and I lived and worked as teachers and afterwards, church leadership. There in that place, remote as well as hot and humid as the wet season worked its patient development of the expected monsoon rain, the reality of Jesus' death and the hope that it brings was immediate to the several hundred mourners who joined in the home, the church and then the cemetery.

Mourning in Kowanyama takes place quite differently from what we might experience in Melbourne. There it is public, protracted and visceral in the combination of wailing and tears as different groups of kin come into the house to sit near the coffin before the funeral service. Encountering death, even of close family members in Western society has become mediated by professionals and, quite often, marked by the repression of any emotional expression of grief. There it is very different, entirely in the hands of the family as soon as the coffin is released from the mortuary. Throughout the whole proceedings that lasted for more than four hours I was the only non-Aboriginal present.

There were several things that struck me during those few days alongside the vividness of the truth of the Ash Wednesday invocation to remember that '... mortal, you are dust and to dust you shall return.' The first was the hope in the resurrection that was spoken about even in the midst of the very visceral expression of grief that I have already mentioned. Even though it is negatively expressed in 1 Thessalonians 4:13, '... do not grieve as others do who have no hope', the combination of such an expression of human grief and Christian hope is powerful. My niece was only in her mid-fifties when she died, the same age as her mother and two of her mother's sisters at the time of their deaths. Her death coming within days of the release of the 'Close the Gap' report gave my reading of this report a very personal reality.

Some of you will have heard me give my opinion that the evangelistic mission of the Church is simply to communicate the Gospel into a new generation and across cultures. Kowanyama was started as an Anglican mission in 1905, in those days it was called Mitchell River Mission. 110 years is not a long time but in that period the role of a public expression of Christian faith and identity has certainly diminished. In Kowanyama, despite many challenges, the expression of the Christian faith is public and certainly central at a time like I have described. Succession of leadership is the next challenge as long-term minsters Father Wayne Connolly and his wife Deacon Val Connolly discern the right time to retire to their home community of Yarrabah.

Please pray for the things I have mentioned here, I know how important it is for Christians in this remote place, that most of us will never experience, to be connected to the concern of the wider church.

March 2018

Walking together, despite our divisions

Jesus in his words in John 8:12 imposes a great responsibility on his followers: 'I am the light of the world. Whoever follows me will never walk in darkness but will have the light of life.' Jesus is talking about his disciples and how they can walk with clear sightedness because of him. Their relationship with Jesus is the foundation for confidence that life can be negotiated with all of its complications and difficult choices.

The danger for Christians is that we can turn this assurance into something that is narrower and focused only on ourselves and our individual opinions. Jesus' assurance in John 8:12 is about the confidence with which we can walk. It is dynamic and certainly far removed from the kind of 'fortress' certainty that we sometimes encounter in the church community.

I think that a good test of the authenticity of our discipleship is whether we are prepared to walk and talk together. Luke 24 gives the account of the walk to Emmaus and how two disciples were walking and talking when Jesus, unapprehended by them, joins them and reveals the light of life.

Let's keep walking and talking together and in that journey grow into a deeper discipleship where we speak and listen with equal measure about the hard things that so easily divide us.

The Emmaus walk ends with Jesus breaking and blessing bread with the two disciples. This was the gestalt moment when 'their eyes were opened' and they recognised Jesus for who he was. Despite this clarity that they had indeed walked in the light with him, 'he vanished from their sight'. I think that this tells us a lot about our walk as disciples and encourages us to keep walking and talking with each other and with our Lord.

May 2018

Honouring George Freier and all the fallen of WWI

As a small child, I was somehow entrusted with a military medal from the First World War. It came to me in a jumble of foreign coins that I now wonder whether they were the souvenirs of various family members' overseas military service. After my family came to Australia in the Nineteenth Century, overseas military service was the only reason anyone ever left Australia. I used to look at this medal with GW Freier, 25 BN AIF engraved around the edge and wonder who and what this was about.

With the centenary of George Freier being killed in action on the Western Front in the First World War drawing near (it falls on 17 July) I have sought better to understand his life and time. I have also tried to make sense of how a generation of Australian parents coped with the death of their sons without the opportunity of the usual rites that assist grieving and mourning. Each First World War honour board I see in the churches I visit emphasises how many families were impacted by the War and how many died amongst those who served. I always ask the present-day parishioners if they recognise the family names listed, either in their congregation or wider community. Very often few or even no names are recognised.

'Lest we forget' is the admonition that is given to us on Anzac Day or Remembrance Day as well as other times that military service and sacrifice is recalled. As time passes it is sure that an increasing number of the individuals listed on honour boards and cenotaphs around the country are not known by us. Perhaps as you read this your own recollection of someone in your family or community is heightened. News of the death of loved ones in the

Great War seems to have been delivered formally and impersonally to the bereaved families. Deprived of the opportunity for funerals back in Australia it is not hard to imagine how bereaved families looked to corporate observance and community memorialisation to make some sense of their loss. Memory is hard to hold and the portrait of George in his military uniform hung on the wall of the local community hall in the small town he came from until recent years. Somehow it had been taken from its frame, the frame taken and the portrait left to the depredations of cockroaches and silverfish until someone picked it up and gave it to my Aunt and then from her to me. More than fifty years of holding his medal and now I find myself holding his portrait as well.

George Freier was a 28-year-old farmer from the hinterland of what is now the Sunshine Coast of Queensland when he enlisted in 1917. He had been on the Western Front from January 1918, over six months, before his death when a shell exploded near him. He is buried in the military cemetery at Villers Brettoneux. It is estimated that four million were killed in the conflicts along the Western Front. These events raise questions about the significance of an individual life and its loss in the midst of such overwhelming carnage. George was also the son of Prussian immigrant families on both his father's and mother's side. Even though they had been in Australia for fifty years by the time of the War, the possible dissonance between citizenship, ethnicity and identity strikes me as, at least, ironic.

If it were not for the firmly formed identity in Christ of many of that generation of families, it is hard to imagine how they could have coped. May our remembrance of these people and times be a holy remembrance from which we learn more of Christ and his grace.

June 2018

From times of crisis, deeper faith can emerge

Moses might be said to have come to a point of crisis when he recovered his identity as a member of the Hebrew people (Genesis 2). From what we know in the verses that deal with his life to that point, he is brought up in both the royal court and in the nurturing presence of his mother. Time goes by and his life seems to be that of the royal circle around Pharaoh, unexceptional until the day of crisis when he takes the side of a Hebrew in a conflict with an Egyptian.

It is not just the decision to take the part of the Hebrew but the escalation of the conflict that sees Moses killing the Egyptian and burying his body in the desert sand. His passion for justice has irrevocably determined the side he would now be on, not that it is uncontended. Only a single day passes until the full impact of what he had decided confronts him. This time two Hebrews are fighting and one, resenting Moses' intrusion, blurts out, 'Who made you a ruler and judge over us? Do you mean to kill me as you killed the Egyptian?' (Genesis 2:14)

Moses is confronted with a brutal reality. He has broken the ties with his former life and is not seeing any early signs that he is on the way to acceptance in the new.

I reflect on this because identity is an important constituent of our contemporary understanding of what it means to be human. Who we are as an individual, how we understand our identity and how our identity is received by others are all relevant to our participation in human community. Whether at mid-life or at other times, 'crisis' is an apt word to describe the position in which many people find themselves. Crisis always implies that we are in a time when we must make a decision and come to a judgment in a time of transition.

Moses resolves his immediate crisis by travelling to Midian and finding purpose and healing in a new family and community. I find the story of Moses a strikingly modern story. Whether it is a 'gap year', a 'tree change' or a 'sea change', or just finding more 'me time', we have institutionalised ways for people to make a better journey through such life transitions and times of crisis than might otherwise be possible.

It is no surprise to me that there is a long tradition of people emerging from crisis with new or deepened Christian faith. Like Moses we need to recognise the full extent of the change we undergo in becoming a Christian and be ready for the implications of that to be worked out in a supportive and nurturing community. Jesus is entirely realistic when he describes how disruptive our discipleship, our following of him may be (Luke 14.26). What seemed settled, even the foundation of our comfort and security, is likely to be radically disrupted by the reality of our Baptism and incorporation into Christ.

May we each, like Moses, find God's deeper purposes in our faithful following of God's call.

July 2019

Seek light, give thanks, don't dwell in shadows

There seems to be a pattern in the affairs of nations that suggests it is the past, not the future – and sometimes not even the present – that dominates approaches to contemporary issues. Examples come readily to mind from world history. Australia's military alliance with the United States is one that was forged in the Pacific theatre of war against Japan. This in turn displaced a reliance on the United Kingdom as Australia's main strategic partner. Even a determination to destroy an old enemy means that new instabilities are formed. The second Gulf War and the invasion of Iraq on the premise of Iraqi military threat readily comes to mind. If we look back further in history, the disintegration of the Austro-Hungarian and Ottoman empires at the end of the First World War has left long shadows that some see reflected in the instability, many years later, in the Balkans and the Middle East.

This is not surprising, especially if the events are so traumatic that they seize attention from other things. Jesus noted something similar in Luke 12 when he encountered the great crowds of people who pressed in on him and the disciples. 'You know how to interpret the appearance of the earth and sky, but why do you not know how to interpret the present time?' The repeated patterns of natural events are easily comprehended in our human wisdom but the exceptional, even the singular, work of God in Jesus was not comprehended with this clarity. Jesus goes on to say in the next verse: 'Why do you not judge for yourselves what is right?' Undoubtedly we are, in our human nature, dull learners. The lack of spiritual insight for which Jesus berates his contemporaries seems well and truly etched in the pages of human history and in the affairs of nations as well.

There are a number of places in the Old Testament where the duration of effects of the failure of one generation on those who come after is described as enduring for 'three or four generations'.

This wisdom was undoubtedly received as applying to individual lives, as we can see in the question the disciples asked Jesus in John 9:2 about the man born blind: 'Rabbi, who sinned, this man or his parents, that he was born blind?', and I think that we can see from Jesus's answer that he did not see it in such a restricted way: 'Neither this man nor his parents sinned; he was born blind so that God's works might be revealed in him.'

There are some spiritual practices that arise out of this biblical perspective. For instance, fostering the growth of our personal thankfulness and gratitude for the many blessings we enjoy is a good place to start. Experienced as a corporate or cultural conviction, this practice would lead to a very different type of public discourse and even politics than we currently experience. Jesus' question 'Why do you not judge for yourselves what is right?' also implies action. Grow your gratitude, keep Jesus in the centre as the focus of your thankfulness and join in to the big thing that God is doing through Christ in our own and every generation.

September 2019

Cosmic calling with Christ
a way ahead on climate

The events of our summer have cast into stark relief our human fragility. Not just the vulnerability of our individual lives in the face of natural disaster, but the very fabric of our society. With roads closed and power and communication lost, whole communities were plunged into survival mode in the bushfire crisis of early January. It is no comfort to realise that the bushfire season can continue well into the year. Australia is experiencing the stretching of the extremes of our environment. Droughts are harder and longer, fires rage with greater intensity, cyclones are more unpredictable and intense. If we ever thought that we lived in a world where we could control the impact of these forces, that assumption has surely been dispelled.

The prescience of the 2008 Garnaut Climate Change review and the failure of our national government to implement action informed by science impels us all to move our debate from opinion to the facts. Internationally, Australia is gaining a bad reputation for its climate scepticism even though we are on track to meet the 2016 Paris targets. Our position at the recent COP25 meeting in Madrid disappointed many when we emphasised relying on carrying over credits from carbon emission reductions under the Kyoto protocol that would result in actual reductions between 2020 and 2030 of only 10% of the Paris target amounts.

I realise that this can all sound technical and even meaningless to the ordinary circumstances of our daily life but is evidence of the 'loophole' positioning that Greta Thunberg named in Madrid. Our Christmas celebrations retell the Biblical narratives about

Jesus' birth and we should not pass over them too lightly or hear them outside of the Biblical narrative of Creation. The Word – or in Greek, the Logos – is present at Creation according to John's Gospel and wonderfully known to us in the person of Jesus the Messiah. In that way, Jesus through his incarnation has a vocation of bringing Creation to its fulfilment and ultimately renewing all things in the new heaven and the new earth. As people gathered into the 'Body of Christ', we have a share in that cosmic vocation. It is a vocation that is relevant to the circumstances of the world at this present time. Carbon dioxide, wherever it comes from, knows no borders and influences the atmosphere and its retention of solar heat equally.

I think that we should not accept arguments that Australia's emissions of carbon are only a small fraction of emissions, and our policies are not significant in the whole. This is an argument that we would never accept if it were applied to drunk drivers or those who suffer from disease. We know in these practical circumstances that policy frameworks that apply to the tiny fraction of occurrences are vital. I suggest that we reframe our climate change debates in Australia to look at the quest from this perspective.

In uncertain times, we can easily despair and lose sight of the mercies of God in both Creation and in Redemption. In these times, it is important that we strengthen both our personal discipleship and our corporate participation as members of the Body of Christ. These are both things that we can do out of our own spiritual discipline and I suggest are vital for us at this time.

Bless you in this year of Grace 2020 and may you know our Saviour's love in the presence of the Holy Spirit.

February 2020

'Forgotten blessings' rediscovered in lockdown

The COVID-19 shutdown has reduced opportunities for activity for all of us. This has not just been an Australian experience but shared throughout the world. It has been an unusual time and one that we are all approaching without lived precedents.

Even the little spaces when things used to slow down, where entertainments and commerce paused for a while, like Good Friday, have been increasingly appropriated as times for ordinary activity to continue. We are a society that seems to aspire to fill all time with as much activity as possible. No wonder the COVID-19 pandemic has been confronting in a society like ours, even if the health impact of the virus has been restrained.

Our society is one where we all seem to share an expectation that something adverse is sure to be able to be 'fixed' by human ingenuity. It is a bit like expecting that there is a scientific, medical or engineering solution to every problem. This anthropocentric view of the world is profoundly different from the worldview of most people who ever lived before us. For most of human existence the role of humanity seemed small when contrasted to natural forces. The ancient wisdom of our culture contains notions that sound eccentric or hyper-religious to many Australians. The idea that the balance of work and rest was ordained in the very fabric of creation, while perceived by those who successfully argued for the eight-hour working day a century ago, is an alien concept for many today.

'And on the seventh day God finished the work that he had done, and he rested on the seventh day from all the work that he had done. So God blessed the seventh day and hallowed it, because on it God rested from all of the work that he had done in creation.' (Genesis 2:2-4) The revelation of the law to Moses further enshrines this principle in the life of the covenant people. The Sabbath day, the Sabbath year and the Jubilee year are all expressions of this creation principle that have shaped our society in one way or another until recent times. We might look to the COVID-19 shutdown as a chance to reset our expectations and as an invitation for us to consider what God intends for us in the post-pandemic world.

The year of Jubilee, part of the divine revelation to Moses in the Book of Leviticus, was an enactment of this creation principle. Coming at the end of seven cycles of seven years, the year of Jubilee was a holy year in which slaves would be freed, debts forgiven, the people restored to their ancestral land and the land itself given a year of rest. How much did the dispossessed and poverty-stricken in Israel long for Jubilee to arrive? It was a once-in-a-lifetime opportunity to reset the circumstances of life for those who had not fared well over the previous 49 years. Wouldn't it be wonderful for this to be the opportunity for our own citizens, those who have become homeless or languish on Manus Island or Nauru?

In saying this I don't under-estimate the real cost of the long lockdown for the economy and its impact on people's lives. Just as many have rediscovered forgotten blessings, both communal and spiritual, in the lockdown there is more for us to reach for as we forge the future of Australian society together.

July 2020

Time for a relevant national anthem

I have been interested to see the national identity debate develop a recent focus on the national anthem. 'Advance Australia Fair' was first performed in 1878, and in its initial context undoubtedly struck a chord with the colonists and their thoughts about the ultimate destiny of the Australian colonies joining together and becoming an independent nation. Most will know how after almost a century in 1977 it was selected as our national song. Symbols are undoubtedly powerful and connect to the emotions. I recall being on the deck of a visiting American warship about 20 years ago and being present when everything stopped as dusk came on and the whole crew turned to salute and watch the 'Stars and Stripes' being lowered from the flag mast for the night as 'Star Spangled Banner' was played. Just this alone seemed to stir a powerful emotional response in my host, one of the senior chaplains, who participated in this ritual solemn and misty eyed. Perhaps the Americans just get this more than I do but I thought at the time that this kind of national piety was not so evident amongst Australians.

Even though 'Advance Australia Fair' was fifty years old at the time of the First World War it still struck a chord amongst the citizens of the now 'young and free' Australia. Recruiting posters of the time showed England as a great full-maned lion surrounded by the now, coming of age, colonial lions ready to take on the fight against the enemy together. If we move on a further 60 years to 1978 there was hardly a Melbourne Cup field of candidates to replace 'God save the Queen'. Hardly surprising either that in the limited field 'Advance Australia Fair' beat 'Waltzing Matilda' in the race to have a more distinctively Australian song as our representative anthem. The truth is, of course, that symbols need to be aligned to reality if they are to be meaningful. On their own, and unattested by the shared identity they represent, they are properly the subject of doubt and questioning.

Around the same period as my visit to the American warship, I had the opportunity of visiting the ancestral home of my father's family in what had become Germany proper but had been East Germany and before that Prussia when my Freier ancestors left there in the 1860's. Visiting the parish church in Brüssow I noticed a related family name on an honour board from the Nineteenth Century commemorating the war dead in some 19th Century Prussian conflict. It caused me to ponder the circumstances of that long dead soldier. Two competing musical narratives informed my reflections. First, the official Prussian anthem from the 1830s onwards, 'Preussenleid' which amongst other flatteries goes, 'The King's call penetrates my heart so deeply; I am a Prussian, want nothing to be but a Prussian.' The second, a folk song 'O König von Preussen', that starts with 'O King of Prussia you mighty man. I've had it with your service, I'm fed up unto here.' You can imagine the contrast of sentiment and perspective! When that gap starts to widen symbols become hollow and potentially divisive.

Let's work to get a society that truly represents the best of our aspirations and not think that we need to rely only on symbols to unify us. Acting now to stop more Australians falling below the poverty line must be an imperative. This includes better investment in social housing and the same determination to reduce homelessness that we saw during our worst days of the pandemic. Surely, we have the creative ability amongst us to tell the identity and aspirations of our times with fresh words and music. The truth is that symbols don't always endure and this is particularly the case for narratives like an anthem. There is no shame or disrespect in retiring them and forging new representations.

November 2020

Thinking about the soul

Evan Osnos' recent book, 'American Dreamer' charts Joe Biden's journey to the US Presidency. A few lines struck me as I read it through. Biden recounts to Osnos a meeting with Russian Prime Minister, Vladimir Putin, 'I said, Mr Prime Minister, I'm looking into your eyes, and I don't think you have a soul ... and he looked back at me, and he smiled, and he said, 'We understand one another." This was interesting as an insight into how high stakes diplomacy occurs but raised the question of the 'soul' and its significance.

We are familiar with soul as a translation for various words in both the Old and New Testaments. Memorable to anyone familiar with the Magnificat is Mary's, 'My soul magnifies the Lord, and my spirit rejoices in God my Saviour.' Here soul and spirit express the 'immaterial' part of the human self in contrast to the body or the flesh. Used together the two words invite a contrast between the soul as the seat of the emotions and the spirit as the seat of the religious life. Some commentators see the different use of these words as a literary device that points back to the same essence of self. There is a beautiful resonance, not just with the Song of Hannah in 1 Samuel 2 but also with Psalm 35:9, 'Then my soul shall rejoice in the LORD, exulting in his deliverance.'

This sense of soul as the 'essence of self' is apparent in 1 Peter 1:9, 'For you are receiving the outcome of your faith, the salvation of your souls.' Some have criticised the 'salvation of souls' language in describing the purpose of the Church's mission on the grounds that it is Platonist and unreasonably contrasts a broken world, mired in sin with the transcendence, even other worldliness of the 'saved soul'. I don't think that objection stands when we take the sense of soul as 'the seat of the emotions'. We quickly circle back to the self as the reality of who are in the world and where our actions arise from the soul in this sense. These actions are evident and display the deeper self and indeed a self that needs salvation.

I'll leave it to Joe Biden and Vladimir Putin to sort out whether the words quoted earlier are an insult from Biden or properly received by Putin as wry praise of his cunning and steely resolve. For our part we are called to recognise that the effect of our faith is transformative and salvific at the deepest level of who we are. Our salvation affects our inner workings at the heart of our emotions and the deepest sense of the spirit within us. The reality of integration of the human person is that our actions and human connections are each fields where our salvation in Christ is at work. It is not so much what we claim for ourselves as the reality of the change that blesses others. We likely feel the effects of our salvation within us but it is in our actions, even the expression of our emotions, that others will experience this reality within us and with God in Christ.

August 2021

No room for complacency

In the preface to his 2012 edition of his biography of Tolstoy, author A.N. Wilson comments about Tolstoy's legacy and his inspiration, 'If we think it is somehow irrational to base our lives on the ethical system of Christ's Sermon on the Mount, maybe we should look again at the world which we have created by ignoring these precepts.' Fifty years earlier, Gerard Tucker, the founder of the Brotherhood of St Laurence expressed similar hopes with typical urgency and passion, hoping that '...before I died, Australia would face up to the world situation as it is, and that all would examine the Gospel as preached by Jesus Christ as if it were something new'. This urgency resulted in his promotion of this idea under the name of the 'Lara Movement' after the location of the St Laurence Village where he lived.

Even though he would go on to live a further nine years after he wrote those words the 80 year old Gerard Tucker was as passionate about the Gospel and its claim on human life as he was in his youth. Tucker hoped to face the big questions of the world like the recurrence of war and the rise of communism with his emphatic Christian faith. He could not make it any plainer that he believed in Jesus Christ as the 'very truth, the Son of God' and he believed as well in 'all that is taught by the Church of his fathers.' The force of the 'Lara Movement' was Tucker's conviction that Christ was capable of transcending all human differences around the rallying cry of his Sermon on the Mount and that there, in the principles of that teaching, 'the Plan' as he called it was plain to see. 'Even the most sceptical', he said 'cannot deny the value of the teaching contained in the Sermon on the Mount – it is universally acknowledged as the most perfect code for human behaviour – but regarding it as an ideal beyond man's attainment and being unable to accept all the teachings of the Church, they reject the whole, out of hand.'

The Sermon on the Mount in Matthew chapters 5 to 7 evokes many responses that arise out of the many topics addressed. Leon Morris considered in his commentary, 'The sermon removes all complacency ... No matter how far we have gone along the Christian road the sermon tells us that there is more ahead of us.' However we look at our life in these present times it is certain that we are seeing a sharper contest of ideas on the global stage and at a local and community level. Globally, the contrast between authoritarianism and democracy is seen more sharply. In our own nation many questions remain as we work our way into shaping life beyond the COVID disruption and as we put into effect carbon emission reduction strategies. Certainly there is no room for any complacency!

There is great space however for the message of Jesus, so clearly gathered by Matthew in his Gospel, to be shared with the world. Lived, spoken and shared - is the living witness we are privileged to make to our Lord and his teaching in our generation and times.

November 2021

Prayers for first steps towards reimagining future

There has been some interesting commentary about the results of the 2021 Census, particularly in respect to religious affiliation. This question is optional but was answered by 93 per cent of those who completed the census. That high response suggests to me that it is a relevant question that Australians have clarity about and about which they are willing to identify their own position. As it has been in previous censuses, Anglicans were the second largest Christian community with about one in 10 Australians identifying as Anglican. Compared with the 2001 census, when Anglicans were 21 per cent of the Australian population, this represents a very significant decrease in terms of the proportion of the total Australian population. Similar declines are recorded in other denominations as well.

Quite apart from the internal dynamics that these changes activate within Australian Anglicanism and many other Christian communities, there is a risk that the decline of Christian identification lessens the engagement of Christians in the public life of our society. It is a paradox that over the past two decades there has been a strong growth of Anglican community service organisations as well as Anglican schools across the country. In Melbourne the financial turnover of our three largest community service organisations, Anglicare, Benetas and the Brotherhood of St Laurence, exceeds that of the diocese, including all of the parishes, by many times. The combined Anglican schools would be greater by another order of magnitude again.

I'm glad that we enjoy a very constructive relationship with our agencies and our colleges and schools. They are separately constituted bodies and seek to interpret their Anglican and Christian character in some very creative ways. Of course they are not the parochial church that is, by and large, the constituent element of the diocese as an organisation. It is in the parishes and authorised Anglican congregations that the foundational responsibility of the church to 'make the Word of God fully known' is exercised. It is vital that we continue to forge strong connections with the congregational life of the Church and its community service and educational organisations.

Back in 2011, I held a conversation in Federation Square called 'Better to give than to receive'. I asserted then that Australian society and public discourse was marked by 'an optimism about a secular ethic, but a doubtfulness about the value of explicitly Christian motivation'. I think that the past decade has confirmed that observation, at least as evidenced in our press and broadcast media. The census figures may well be further evidence of this disposition.

We are embarking on a further stage of our 'Reimagining the Future' project. The first step was to offer resources to each of our parishes; this next step will be to work more intensively with a cohort of around 30 parishes that have emerged out of COVID with significant challenges to their ministry vitality. At the heart of this work is the conviction that the life-giving power of the gospel to transform human life is as important to our society as it ever was. God's faithfulness exceeds our human response, we will always be faced with the reality of this gap.

In some seasons the headwinds of secularism and even cynicism about faith seem greater but I suspect that every generation has needed to face the fact of its unique task of proclaiming the gospel in its own cultural context. If the census is any guide, contemporary evangelism will be met with clear views about religion and religious people. Some of these views will be unsympathetic or perhaps even hostile. Notwithstanding this possibility, it is vital that we are out and visible in our community, engaging with people and not retreating into sectarian isolation. Pray for the next steps of 'Reimagining the Future' and for our combined Christian witness in the world around us.

August 2022

On our doors, at our tables, we can share God's gift to us

Our Advent pilgrimage to Christmas calls for us to prepare our hearts for the celebration of the incarnation of the Messiah.

We can make this pilgrimage in different ways. In churches where an Advent wreath is used to evoke a theme of hope, faith, joy and peace we can carry that reflection into our own homes and light a candle throughout the weekdays that follow. As we light a candle in our own place, the prayer of the previous Sunday can be prayed as we move deeper into that spiritual grace that is commended for our reflection that week.

Even stepping outside, contemplating the night sky, and praying 'Lord what gift do I bring to you?' may serve to evoke the Journey of the Magi as an inspiration for your own pilgrimage. I've been told that people used to rely on hearing the Collect for the Sunday before Advent 'Stir up, we beseech thee, O Lord, the wills of thy faithful people' as a prompt to make their Christmas puddings. However we connect words and actions, it is clear that our Christian faith is an embodied and not just an abstract conviction.

This is hardly surprising as the Incarnation of our Lord is God coming amongst us, 'taking the form of a servant, assuming human likeness' (Philippians 2:7). In that passage, we are encouraged to 'Let the same mind be in you that was in Christ Jesus'. Our gift of imagination, our use of symbols and associating them with the language of prayer is a powerful means for us each to enter fresh spiritual experiences within the familiar yearly round.

If the enthusiastic adoption of Halloween by many Australians is anything to go by, there is an openness to symbolic enactments in our community. It may be that the Advent wreath can become that kind of reminder in our neighbourhoods that Christmas is coming but even more so that 'every tongue should confess that Jesus Christ is Lord, to the glory of God the Father'. On our doors or at our table there is the opportunity that we can, through word and symbol, share the hope, faith, joy and peace that is God's gift to us in Christ.

I hope that you will come to a joyful celebration of Christmas. With the psalmist we will, 'Sing to the Lord a new song, for he has done marvellous things'. Jesus was born into a broken world and lives for the restoration of all that is marred by those old sins that have broken the heart and peace of humanity. Violence and hatred among them, have long beset our world. 'The Lord remembers his mercy and faithfulness to the house of Israel, and all the ends of the earth have seen the victory of our God.' (Psalm 98)

December 2022

Contemplating the divine vision of Jubilee

It is very easy to see the demands on infrastructure investment as we drive around Melbourne or Geelong. New roads, schools and hospitals are obviously needed to meet the basic needs of a growing population. The costs of infrastructure are enormous, $1.5 billion for the New Footscray Hospital, over $12 billion for the Metro rail tunnel project, and the West Gate road tunnel predicted to cost $10 billion. Even the cost of changing policy is great, the cancellation of the East West Link project in June 2015 cost over $400 million. And these are just the capital costs. Schools and hospitals need staffing and the provision of other services to maintain their operations.

It is not hard to see the pressure on state and federal sources of taxation income and the challenges in finding the balance between raising income and spending. There is a balance too that must be reached between these sorts of capital items, including defence spending for the Commonwealth, and the investments in services and people that are needed. This is a live question at the present time, whether the funds designated to build a new stadium in Hobart are better spent on investing in public housing as that state experiences great pressure in adequately housing its people.

We often hear the word 'crisis' applied to one side or other of the debate about where our public resources are best applied and in what priority. As far as I can tell these debates happen in similar ways, with perhaps different questions, in most countries. Internationally this meets various responses, whether through higher taxes or greater expectation of non-government solutions or even tolerating widening inequality between rich and poor.

The Bible gives us the wonderful vision of Jubilee as an extrapolation of the principle of Sabbath. After the passing of 'seven weeks of seven years', the fiftieth year was a time of rest for the fields but more importantly for restoration of birthright for those who had experienced hard times, indebtedness, and thus loss of dignity and social standing. It was the ultimate disrupter to 'inter-generational disadvantage'. Probably regarded as simplistic and unrealistically idealistic in today's politics, it is a powerful divine vision for us to grapple with as we seek to name a Christian response within the many debates about contended, and even competing, priorities.

As we approach the 80th anniversary of the death of William Temple in 2024 it would be fruitful to open again his *Christianity and Social Order*. This short book, written in 1941, integrated the ancient wisdom of God's revelation with the emerging challenges that Temple could see arising after wartime. Temple was keen to establish the principles by which policy could be judged, rather than to advocate for distinctive policies themselves. I look forward to Temple's thoughts being freshly explored as we approach this anniversary. His work is important in integrating the biblical witness with the questions of equity and justice that arise in the context of pressure on our social security system, Medicare and NDIS. May the vision of Jubilee inform our prayers for our world and its people.

June 2023

Abide in Jesus, not outrage culture

While the memory of the second cricket Test at Lord's in the Ashes series has likely receded from our attention, we may still recall the controversy over the dismissal of English batter, Jonny Bairstow that seized media attention at the time. As John Silvester wrote in the Age newspaper, '... this is the modern world where outrage is the new international currency. Where being mean is a substitute for being strong. Any fool can yell insults. Only the wise see both sides. Both British and Australian PMs have weighed into the Bairstow debate as if it actually matters. You would think they both would have more important things to do.'

Unsurprisingly, the Wisdom literature of the Bible contains many references to this same phenomenon. Our trajectory towards being outraged may seem modern but is in fact a well-trodden, even if unproductive, path. 'Refrain from anger and forsake wrath. Do not fret – it only leads to evil.' (Psalm 37:8) and 'Do not be quick to anger, for anger lodges in the bosom of fools.' (Ecclesiastes 7:9).' Both of these verses come to mind from the Old Testament as does 2 Timothy 2:23 amongst many other references in the New Testament, 'Have nothing to do with stupid and senseless controversies; you know they breed quarrels.'

Even though we are well warned about the unproductiveness of outrage it nonetheless seems very attractive, especially when it becomes a shared societal response. It can seem that the proposition is that, if something really matters it properly should call us to express that conviction with unattenuated intensity. Jesus receives that kind of response when the crowd calls out 'Crucify him'. In his pastoral ministry, the same response is seen in the accusation that he was 'a glutton and a drunkard, a friend of tax collectors and sinners!' (Matthew 11:19). Jesus goes on to say in response to this accusation that, 'Wisdom is vindicated by her deeds.'

As John Silvester said, 'Any fool can yell insults. Only the wise see both sides.' Foolishness inevitably invites the contrast to wisdom. Foolishness is easily embraced but wisdom arises out of the disciplining, or as we might better say, the discipling of the mind and the heart. John's Gospel tells us that Jesus made the connection between discipleship and abiding in his word. 'If you abide in my word, you are truly my disciples, and you will know the truth, and the truth will set you free.' (John 8:31, 32) This is powerful and succinct language and, as Jesus elaborates later in the Fourth Gospel, at the very heart of the question of how his disciples live in the world. Speaking of his forthcoming death Jesus says, 'I have said this to you, so that in me you may have peace. In the world you face persecution. But take courage; I have conquered the world.' (John 16:33)

May you find the peace that is Jesus' gift to all who follow him. May you also be protected from the unproductive temptation to join in the responses of the 'crowd' and instead abide in Jesus' love.

August 2023

The Yoorook Justice Commission and our Diocese's painful history

The Yoorook Justice Commission was established by the Victorian Government with details published in the Victoria Government Gazette on 14 May 2021. It is an important commission with the powers of a Royal Commission. Yoorook has wide terms of reference that include enquiring into 'Historical Systemic Injustice ...since the start of Colonisation' along with 'Ongoing Systemic Injustice' in a range of areas including youth and criminal justice, child protection, health and welfare. Suffice it to say that the scope of the Commission's responsibilities is quite broad.

The Anglican, Uniting and Catholic Churches in Victoria were recently requested to prepare responses to a range of questions from the Commission in preparation for their participation in a panel discussion that met with the Commissioners on 1 May this year. Amongst the concerns of the Commission was the question of land being gifted to Churches in the colonial period of Victoria as 'Crown Grants'. The Commission was also interested in the churches' history and involvement with missions to Aboriginal people during that same period.

It is certainly the case that the history of colonisation has been repeatedly told from the perspective of the colonists and not from the First Nations people whom the colonists inevitably and systematically drove from their land and traditional life. The colonial enterprise inexorably expanded to cover the whole of, what is now, the State of Victoria as it did over different periods in other parts of Australia. There were certainly members of the Church of England who denounced the injustice of what was happening as there must surely been amongst its members those who were perpetrators of that injustice. Being an intergenerational community that has a strong value of presence in community inevitably means that we have an intertwined history with all that has gone before us in our State.

Great atrocities were committed against First Peoples in this period of frontier expansion and, to the extent that we remain ignorant about it, we compound the consequences of that injustice in our own day. Bishop Richard Treloar and Bishop Genieve Blackwell participated in the 1 May panel on behalf of the Anglican Province of Victoria and I am grateful for their sensitive and courageous witness to this painful history. In his opening statement to the Commission, the Bishop of Gippsland lamented that, 'the colonial history includes atrocities committed against First Peoples and that some of those involved in the heinous, but no longer unspeakable, acts, are likely to have identified with the Church of England.' He went on to say that the Church has 'been complicit in, and has benefitted from, the dispossession and other harms caused by Victoria's colonisation, legitimated in part by the theologically repugnant (and now repudiated) 'doctrine of discovery', and its outworking in the morally bankrupt ideology of *terra nullius*.'

I commend the work of the Yoorook Commission to your attention and your prayers. The Commission is carrying out important work to better understand the past and to recommend policies to the State Government for a better, and reconciled, future. While I suspect that it is not receiving the press coverage that it deserves there is much information on its website including on the panel discussion already referred to.

June 2024

Love of neighbour

A little more than a generation ago, the fall of the Berlin Wall in 1989 and the dissolution of the Soviet Union in 1991 seemed to prefigure the triumph of democracy over totalitarianism. Hopes were embraced that other places would embrace democracy and reject the rule of military or party 'strongmen'. The 'Arab Spring' that started with the forced resignation of the Tunisian president early in 2011 swept through North Africa and the Middle East over the next few years. Responses were complex, with some societies fragmenting into warring groups, others enduring foreign intervention and all causing a massive refugee crisis.

Stability has returned to some countries like Egypt as a result of a military coup. The unrest has continued, with great cost to human life, in Yemen, Libya and Syria and most recently conflict has resumed in Sudan. A wider scan across the globe would reveal its own story but the optimism of the triumph of democracy that was imagined in late 80s and early 90s seems far less certain now than it did then.

On the positive side for democracy there have been successful elections in India, South Africa and Indonesia. Given that between them they constitute over 21% of the world's population, that is a weighty counterbalance to the failures of democratic aspiration elsewhere. If the recent elections for the European Parliament are added, 30% of the world's population have expressed their democratic choice just in these four polls. Democracy still faces headwinds in many places, even in the USA, the country that has long claimed to be its greatest exponent. Time will tell whether popularists make a headway in the forthcoming elections in France and the United Kingdom and what will be the result in the Biden

Trump Presidential rerun. Are the seeds of democratic aspiration only dormant in China, awaiting for the right time to flourish or has the heavy hand of the party eliminated them entirely?

Should any of this matter to Christians? After all, Christianity found its first legal acceptance in the Byzantine Court, hardly an example of democracy. While Christians have endured and even flourished under all kinds of human social organisation, it is at least arguable that our modern expressions of democracy are influenced by important Christian principles. The link between Aristotle and St Thomas Aquinas is often made to account for concepts like the 'common good' and the necessity of the governed to ultimately consent to those who govern them. Reformation thinkers reshaped the social value and thus political importance of the individual with their emphasis on the immediacy between the Christian believer and sacred scripture.

The words of Jeremiah 29 '... seek the welfare of the city where I have sent you into exile, and pray to the LORD on its behalf, for in its welfare you will find your welfare', speaks to a generous theological tradition spanning several millennia. Democracy is part of this generous response of faith-filled people to the world around them, an expression, in Jesus' words of 'Love of neighbour'.

May I encourage you to pray for the welfare of your neighbourhood and city.

July 2024

www.ingramcontent.com/pod-product-compliance
Lightning Source LLC
Chambersburg PA
CBHW011127070526
44584CB00028B/3810